NEVER

ALSO BY JORIE GRAHAM

HYBRIDS OF PLANTS AND OF GHOSTS

EROSION

THE END OF BEAUTY

REGION OF UNLIKENESS

MATERIALISM

THE BEST AMERICAN POETRY 1990, EDITOR

THE DREAM OF THE UNIFIED FIELD: SELECTED POEMS 1974–1994

EARTH TOOK OF EARTH:
100 GREAT POEMS OF THE ENGLISH LANGUAGE, EDITOR

POEMS AND PHOTOGRAPHS
(WITH JEANETTE MONTGOMERY BARRON)

THE ERRANCY

SWARM

NEVER

POEMS

Jorie Graham

ecco

An Imprint of HarperCollinsPublishers

HarperCollins books may be purchased for educational, business, or sales promotional use.
For information please write: Special Markets Department,
HarperCollins Publishers Inc., 10 East 53rd Street, New York, NY 10022.

First Ecco paperback edition published 2003

DESIGNED BY FEARN CUTLER DE VICQ

The Library of Congress has catalogued the hardcover edition as follows:

Graham, Jorie, 1951-
Never : poems / Jorie Graham.—1st ed.
p. cm.
ISBN 0-06-008471-5 (hardcover)
I. Title

PS3557.R214 N38 2002
811'.54—dc21
2001051279

ISBN 0-06-008472-3 (pbk.)

03 04 05 06 07 ❖/RRD 10 9 8 7 6 5 4 3 2 1

This book is for Emily

Grateful acknowledgment to the editors of the following magazines and journals in which these poems (sometimes in altered form, or with different titles) first appeared: *The New Yorker, Conjunctions, The Kenyon Review, Denver Quarterly, Fence, Jubilat, Harvard Magazine,* the *New York Times* (Op-Ed page), the *New York Times Magazine, Boston Review, Countermeasures, Seneca Review, London Review of Books, The Times Literary Supplement, Volt, The American Poetry Review.*

A few of the poems were printed, in different versions in some cases, in a fine-press limited edition titled *All Things,* from the University of Iowa's Center for the Book. My thanks to Shari deGraw and Brien Woods.

"Evolution" ("How old are you?") was written on commission for the *New York Times Magazine* in response to a survey of American public sentiment at the close of the millennium. My thanks to David Shipley.

"Gulls" also appeared in *The Best American Poetry 2000* (ed. Robert Hass).

Some of this work was written for the Environmental Protection Agency, for use in a collaboration with the sculpture of Beverly Pepper.

A number of these poems were written on commission for the National Millennium Survey Project, in conjunction with the College of Santa Fe. My thanks to the whole organization, and to Greg Glazner in particular.

My gratitude, as well, to Robert Whiting (in Todos Santos), and Lila Stine (in Chilmark).

CONTENTS

"How can I believe in that? Surely it cannot be?"

John Keats, 1818

(upon first viewing the scenery of the Lake District)

I

PRAYER

Over a dock railing, I watch the minnows, thousands, swirl
themselves, each a minuscule muscle, but also, without the
way to *create* current, making of their unison (turning, re-
                                        infolding,
entering and exiting their own unison in unison) making of themselves a
visual current, one that cannot freight or sway by
minutest fractions the water's downdrafts and upswirls, the
dockside cycles of finally-arriving boat-wakes, there where
they hit deeper resistance, water that seems to burst into
itself (it has those layers), a real current though mostly
invisible sending into the visible (minnows) arrowing
                        motion that forces change—
this is freedom. This is the force of faith. Nobody gets
what they want. Never again are you the same. The longing
is to be pure. What you get is to be changed. More and more by
each glistening minute, through which infinity threads itself,
also oblivion, of course, the aftershocks of something
at sea. Here, hands full of sand, letting it sift through
in the wind, I look in and say take this, this is
what I have saved, take this, hurry. And if I listen
now? Listen, I was not saying anything. It was only
something I did. I could not choose words. I am free to go.
I cannot of course come back. Not to this. Never.
It is a ghost posed on my lips. Here: never.

AFTERWARDS

I am beneath the tree. To the right the river is melting the young sun.

And translucence itself, bare, bony, feeding and growing on the manifest,

frets in the small puddles of snowmelt sidewalks and frozen lawns hold up

full of sky.

From this eternity, where we do not resemble ourselves, where

resemblance is finally

beside (as the river is) the point,

and attention can no longer change the outcome of the gaze,

the ear too is finally sated, starlings starting up ladderings of chatter,

all at once all to the left,

invisible in the pruned-back

hawthorn, heard and heard again, and yet again

differently heard, but silting

the head with inwardness and making always a

dispersing but still

coalescing opening in the listener who

cannot *look* at them exactly,

since they are invisible inside the greens—though screeching-full in

syncopations of yellowest,

fine-thought, finespun

rivering of almost-knowables. "Gold" is too dark. "Featherwork"

too thick. When two

appear in flight, straight to the child-sized pond of

melted snow,

and thrash, dunk, rise, shake, rethrashing, reconfiguring through

reshufflings and resettlings the whole body of integrated

featherwork,

they shatter open the blue-and-tree-tip filled-up gaze of

the lawn's two pools,

breaking and ruffling all the crisp true sky we had seen living

down in that tasseled

earth. How shall we say this *happened?* Something inaudible

has ceased. Has gone back round to an other side

of which this side's access was [is] this width of sky

deep in

just-greening soil? We left the party without a word.

We did not change, but time changed us. It should be,

it seems, one or the other of us who is supposed to say—lest

there be nothing—*here we are.* It was supposed to become familiar

(this earth). It was to become "ours." Lest there be nothing?

Lest we reach down to touch our own reflection here?

Shouldn't depth come to sight and let it in, in the end, as the form

the farewell takes: representation: dead men:

lean forward and look in: the raggedness of where the openings

are: precision of the limbs upthrusting down to hell:

the gleaming *in*: so blue: and that it *has* a bottom: even a few clouds

if you keep

attending: and something that's an *edge-of*: and mind-cracks: and how the

poem is

about that: that distant life: I carry it inside me but

can plant it into soil: so that it becomes impossible

to say that anything swayed

from *in* to *out*: then back to "is this mine, or yours?": the mind

seeks danger out: it reaches in, would touch: where the subject is emptying,

war is:

morality play: preface: what there is to be thought: love:

begin with the world: let it be small enough.

PHILOSOPHER'S STONE

It's like this. There are quantities. There's on-
                   goingness—
no—there's an underneath. Over it we lay
time—actually more like takes and re-
                   takes by
the mind (eyes closed) then clickings of
its opening-out and the mind fills
with gazes—thousands over some visualizations—or some
places if you wish—I wish—a few or no gazes over some
(because somewhere there must be a meadow with just such
                       grasses
no gaze has touched)—(because it *is*
touch)—(and other places where millions have laid down
their mental waters in this manner). Above and
below our gaze, I don't know for sure—although I
believe there must be a truth—gravity lays,
is laid, in—like a color being washed over
the whole—a tint with a direction in it—
or rather a tint that places tiny arrowings,
or the sensation of pulling of being pulled over
all of the visualization—eyes open now—over
sky, blue, stonewall, vectoring grasses, three trees,
distance, close-up—all as if
being drawn-in without it affecting *how*.
If you open and close your eyes
there should be a difference, no, in the way
the thing seen *is*—in its weight?—and then

what the thinking has begun to make—which is
not the tint of gravity, nor the *was* of the ticking,
(what's not there if we leave
altogether for example)—because there is, on it, which we've
                                             somehow
introduced, this wash which is duration, a very
sturdy though of course not touchable fabric, and because
we can creep along it—or simply
count lengths back—because because of it there *is* a "back"—
not a *back* on the field itself but a back to the
thinking—which *does* begin now to apprehend the edges of
skeletal diminuendos of glancings as they
ascend the manifest up towards its upper reaches—soil,
timothy, stone, manyness of stone, non-mortared
                         build-up of it—
mistings of just-above-stone where the
two of them meet, manifest, un-manifest [and how they
                              could not
know who was looking at them][and that I was from
another country][down to the very movement of my lips]
[show me a word I can use][and how all that you say
is taken from you, they take it, just like
that, it becomes smoke] smoke rising here as mist off the heavy
                              topmost stones
of the wall, raised so carefully up from the field,
to make this edge of precarious positionings,
that make the suddenly-green silence actually hold still, hold
                         up—a kind of trophy
to property, to the property of gravity—a waltz
of motions (fallings, tumblings) stilled—

a thing of number without a numbering—as if every

                  movement

of some gathering crowd's lips were, having uttered each one

                             their one

request, cast forth into manifestation—slightly round with

syllable then placed—a long wall of requests so carefully placed—

each almost pitiful with fear and desire—from each request the soil

                  scraped-off—

                  where it's dug-up—

from the wide field it now defines—the hole

filling back in on itself—as the self fills in on itself—a

                  collectivity—a

god making of himself many

creatures [in the cage there is food][outside only the great

circle called freedom][an empire which begins

with a set table] and I should like, now that the last washes of my gaze

let loose over the field, to say, of this peering,

it is the self—there—out to the outer reaches of

my hand, holding it out before me now, putting it into where

my breath begins to whitely manifest my difference to

night air: look: it is a law: the air

draws on itself the self's soft temperature:

it looks like rain: there is a beforehand: I brought

my life from it thus far: moments are attached.

The nets of the glance draw in. Some

admixture is caught. Some not. There is

impatience but not in the self alone. The open

has its own impatience. The edges fill with it

there where a voice is raised.

Anticipation pulls one way. Regret the other.

A smile can open or close the face. Blood

is almost touchable by sun. Footsteps bent the grass

                                        a bit

to get us here. Looking behind
I see the lift in the bent weeds, I see in them
what cannot be conceived of—quite—I see *it* rise, erasing
path. As where a hand
clutches a wound, tightly, stanching the blood.
Why did we take this way? Where does this *going*
go? Maybe it can bend down now and shut its hand
over a stone. To toss it hard across the field. To have it
land somewhere. Exactly. Yes. Somebody
loves you. Elsewhere a people now is being forced
from home. Looking out, as dusk comes on,
no looking up or down anymore.
Everything taken in as stone by grass.
Does one know
what one likes. What one is like. What is a feeling
in the heart. What troubles
the soul. What troubles the jonquils nearest me
as the light, the cage of this,
goes out. What is it that can now
step *out*. And is the open door through me.
Beyond us now, close-in, nearby,
how near I cannot tell, around us, in us, near: the
sensation of beauty unseen; an owlet's

                        cry;

a cry from something closer to the ground that's uttered
twice and which I cannot name—although it
seems bright yellow in its pitch.

WOODS

O stubborn appetite: *I*, then *I*,

loping through the poem. Shall I do that again?

Can we put our finger on it?

These lines have my breathing in them, yes.

Also my body was here. Why try to disguise it.

In this morning of my year

that will never be given back.

Also those who will not give it back. Whoever they

                                       may be.

How quietly they do their job

over this page. How can I know when it's the

case—oh swagger of dwelling in place, in voice—

surely one of us understands the importance.

Understands? Shall I wave a "finished" copy at you

whispering do you wish to come for lunch.

Nor do I want to dwell on this.

I cannot, actually, dwell on this.

There is no home. One can stand out here

and gesture wildly, yes. One can say "finished"

and look *into* the woods, as I do now, here,

but also casting my eye out

to see (although that was yesterday)(in through the alleyways

of trees) the slantings of morninglight

(speckling)(golden) laying in

these foliate patternings, this goldfinch, this

suddenly dipping through and rising to sit very still

on top of the nearest pine, big coin, puffed-out,

little hops and hopes when he turns, sometimes
                                    entering into
full sun—becoming yellowest then—these line
                            endings
branching out too only so far
hoping for the light of another's gaze to pan them,
as the gaze pans for gold in day, a day sometimes overcast,
                                    but what
would the almost-gold (so that I can't
say "golden") bird be but your eye?
Do not harm him. I can bring him back,
and the way he hopped, turning, on the topmost spike
of the pine—how many minutes
ago was it I said "golden"—and does he still linger there
turning chest into and out of the story, hot singular,
not able to shed light off himself yet so
                full of my
                glance—me
running on something that cripples me—
do not harm him, do not touch him, don't probe
with the ghost your mind this future as it lays itself out
here, right over the day, straight from the font, and yes
I *am* afraid, and yes my fear is
flicking now from limb to limb, swooping once completely out of
sight—oh flickering long corridor—then
                            back,
the whole wind-sluiced avenued continuum taking
my eye around in it—who could ever hold so many
thoughts in mind—him back now, back, my fear,
and my mind gathering wildly up to still itself on him.

IN / SILENCE

I try to hold my lie in mind.

My thinking one thing while feeling another.

My being forced. Because the truth

is a thing one is not permitted to *say*.

That it is reserved for silence,

a buttress in silence's flyings, its motions

always away from source; that it is re-

served for *going* too, for a deeply

artifactual spidery form, and how it can, gleaming,

yet looking still like mere open air, mere light,

catch in its syntax the necessary sacrifice.

Oh whatever that might be. How for song

I looked today long and hard at a singing bird,

small as my hand, inches from me, seeming

to puff out and hold something within, something that

                                 makes

wind ruffle his exterior more—watched

him lift and twist a beak sunlight made burnt-silver

as he tossed it back—not so much to let

anything *out* but more to carve and then to place firmly in the

                                 listening space

                                 around him

a piece of inwardness: no visible

passaging-through: no inner complication and release:

no passage from an inner place—a mechanism

of strings, bone, hollow

chamber—no native immaterial quiver time turns material—

then towards [by mechanisms ancient and invisible] expression,
and the tragic of all upward motion—
then it all lost in the going aloft with the as yet

unsung—then

the betrayal (into the clear morning air)
of the source of happiness into mere (sung) happiness.
Although there is between the two, just at the break
of silentness, a hovering, almost a penitent

hesitation, an

intake, naked, before any dazzling release
of the unfree into the seeming free, and it seems
it goes elsewhere, and the near (the engine) overruns
into the truly free. This till the last stars be counted?
This plus the mind's insistent coming back and coming back?
This up against that coming back. The death of
uncertainty. The song that falls upon the listener's *eye,*
that seeks the sleek minimum of the meaningless *made.*
Here in the morning light. In matter's massive/muscular/venerable holding-in
of all this flow. Next door the roses flow.
Blood in the hand that reaches for them flows.

PRAYER

Am I still in the near distance
where all things are overlooked
if one just passes by. Do you pass
                      by?
I love the idea of consequence.
Is that itself consequence—(the idea)?
I have known you to be cheap
(as in not willing to pay out the extra
                    length of
blessing, weather, ignorance—all other
[you name them] forms of exodus).
What do I (call) you after all the necessary
                 ritual and protocol
is undertaken? Only-diminished?
Great-and-steady-perishing? Unloosening
                       thirst,
or thirst unloosening ribbony storylines
                   with births
and history's ever-tightening
              plot
attached? We're in too deep the bluebird
              perched on
              the seaweed-colored
limb (fringed with sky as with ever-lightening echoes of
            those selfsame light-struck weeds, those
            seas)

seems to be chattering at me. Too deep?

Someplace that is all speech?

Someplace everything can be said to be

about?

Will we all know if it's blindness, this

way of seeing

when it becomes

apparent? Is there, in fact [who could

tell me

this?] a

we? Where? The distances have everything in their

grip of

in-betweenness.

For better [she said] or for worse [he said]

taking their place alongside the thirst

in line, something vaguely audible about

the silence

(a roar

actually)(your sea at night) but not as

fretful nor as monstrously tender

as the sea wind-driven was

earlier on

in "creation." Oh creation!

What a mood that was. Seeding then dragging-up life and

death in swatches

for us to forage in. Needle, story, knot, the

knot bit off,

the plunging-in of its silvery proposal,

stitch stitch still clicks

the bird still on

its limb, still in the mood, at the very edge

of the giddy

woods

through which even this sharpest noon must

bleed, ripped into

flickering bits.

But it is nothing compared to us

is it, that drip and strobe of the old-world's

gold

passaging-through,

nothing bending its forwardness, nothing

being bent

by it (though the wind, rattling the whole business,

would make one think

it so). Nothing

compared. And yet it is

there, truly there, in all sizes, that dry

creation—

woods, dappling melancholias of singled-out

limb-ends, lichened trunk-

flanks—shocked

transparencies as if a rumor's just passed

through

leaving this trail of inconclusive

trembling bits of some

momentous story.

Was it true, this time, the rumor?

The wherefore of our being here?

Does it *come* true in the retelling?

and truer in

the re-presenting? It looks like laughter as the

wind picks up and the blazing is tossed

from branch to branch, dead bits, live

                              bits,

new growth taking the light less brightly than

the blown-out lightning-strikes. Look:

it is as if you are remembering

                    the day

you were born. The *you*. The newest witness. Bluish then

                                    empurpling then

pink and ready to begin continuing.

Lord of objects. Lord of bleeding and self-

                    expression.

I keep speaking this to you, as if in pity

at the gradual filling of the vacancy

by my very own gaze etcetera. Also the

words—here and here—hoping

this thing—along with all else that

                    wears-out—will

                    do. I think

about you. Yet is only *thinking* omnipresent?

Omniscience, omnipotence: that is all drama.

But omnipresence: time all over the

                    place!

It's like a trance, this time unspooling in

                          this telling.

Like land one suspects must be there, but where?

The ocean kisses every inch of the seeable.

We live. We speak at the horizon. After a

                    while even the

                    timidity

wears off. One speaks. One is not mad.
One lives so long one feels the *noticing*

             in all one sees.

             Years. Chapters.

Someone is asking for your hand. One turns

                 to speak.

One wishes so one could be interrupted.

II

EVOLUTION

How old are you?

As old as until now.

Under the kelp-bed razorclams turning to find

                        purchase.

Young things shooting first-times and retaining

                        precedence.

Razors digging backwards and down,

spurting spittle-bits of sea

to equalize descent.

Do you believe that after you die some part of you

                        lives on?

Do you pray in hope of reward?

Do you agree or disagree with the following

                        statement:

it bothers me my life did not turn out as I

                        expected.

Also there are people on the beach.

And wind accepted by waterfilm.

Look: acceptance has a shape.

And fate—is it accepted by waterfilm?

And how we must promise things.

Do you pray in hope of reward.

Do you pray without hope of reward.

What is it has been gone a long time?

How long is the slightest chance?

Everything in sunlight

improvising backwards,

scratching phrases in a rapid jitter,

where the mind above it begins, ends, tries to get up

                              and move

towards or away from.

You'll feel the so-called music strut hard against

                      the downsuck.

Also someone's shadow going to purchase a beverage.

Also everything in sunlight trying to become bodied by something

                                    else,

the whole retreating ocean laying

microscopic and also slightly larger fiercely-lit

kelp in streaks of action—

long sentences with branchlike off-widths indicating

                acceleration brought forth

and left-off, phrases of gigantic backing-off

            from a previously

held shore,

      rivulets of sand left visible in raised inscription

whitening where moistened—questionlike—algebraic—

regarding the long leave-taking—

We are ourselves walking to the right.

The noon hour is itself always a firstness

           of something.

Also, elsewhere, who is hungry?

How small are they? How? I step on parts of

faces, only parts. A whole face, what is that? From here

it seems hard to make out, also a very empty

thing. Like the border of a nationstate.

Being comes into this, idles,

over the interminable logic of

manyness, the demand that *something exist.*

Bending to look close, a

spiking-up and forth of burrowings,

channelings, a turning, a re-turning on

itself where the broad

nouns of large clamshells

flayed open by gulls lie

in punctuating sunlit stillness

on top of a thing which but for

their stillness and expulsion

has no top. The seagulls

hurrying, dragging and retrieving. Also

pecking in place and dropping and

lifting. Sometimes stepping backwards in order to

drag and loosen. Also the drag of the slantline

downtilted towards ocean's sucking further still of

streams of water towards

itself. Of course the future

wasn't there before at all.

This all first time and then again first

> time.

I feel reproach. Eyes closed I touch my face.

My hand hovers like the very question of my face

> over my face.

G says, breathing beside me, that firstness is not, in any case,

a characteristic of experience.

He speaks of the long chain back

to the beginning of "the world" (as he calls it) and then, at last,

> to the great *no*

beginning. I feel the *no* begin.

Subsequence hums tinily all round me,

erasing my tracks. Oh bright/morning. This

                        morning.

Look: what looks like retreating is not exactly so.

Sunlight makes of exactness an issue.

No issuing *forth* of matter

because of sunlight. But sun's

up-sucking also at work. And how

it seems to have weight,

pushing the originally pillowy kelp-beds

down, flattening them where they

give up water, unthickening their

pastures as the tunneling-away from

that gigantic drying drives

the almost-imperceptible downwards:

first glitter then more unchangeable shine slowly being

forced into the vast top of the

beachwide beds. Drying out and

hardening, the beds force light

                  back.

Back across what resides inside.

White closed-in part of gazing-out.

Bothered by the ease of touch.

As if one should open out and spill, again.

Sound in the sun now muted

(is there an inherent good)

as the ruffling back-roar recedes

(is there inherent good in people)—

Sound becoming particular and pricked

with syncopations of singularities—
peeps, insucks, snaps—where light is
                              in domain.
What good is my silence for, what would it hold
                              inside, keeping it free?
Sing says the folding water on stiller water—
one running through where the other's breaking. Sing me
something (the sound of the low wave-breaking)
(the tuning-down where it deposits life-matter on
the uphill of shore)(also the multiplicity
of deepenings and coverings where whiteness rises as a
                                        manyness)
(as the wave breaks over its own breaking)
(to rip in unison)(onto its backslide)—
of something sing, and singing, disagree.

GULLS

Those neck-pointing out full bodylength and calling
outwards over the breaking waves.
Those standing in waves and letting them come and
                              go over them.
Those gathering head-down and over some one
                                   thing.
Those still out there where motion is
primarily a pulsing from underneath
and the forward-motion so slight they lay
their stillness on its swelling and falling
and let themselves swell, fall...
Sometimes the whole flock rising and running just
as the last film of darkness rises
leaving behind, also rising and falling in
                        tiny upliftings,
almost a mile of white underfeathers, up-turned, white spines
                                gliding over the wet
sand, in gusts, being blown down towards
                 the unified inrolling awayness
                 of white. All things turning white through
breaking. The long red pointing of lowering sun
going down on (but also streaking in towards) whoever
might be standing at the point-of-view place
from which this watching. This watching being risen
from: as glance: along the red
blurring and swaying water-path:
to the singular redness: the glance a

being-everywhere-risen-from: everywhere
cawing, mewing, cries where a
single bird lifts heavily
just at shoreline, rip where
its wing-tips (both) lap
backwash, feet still in
the wave-drag of it, to coast
on top of its own shadow and then down to not
landing.

*

Also just under the wave a thickening where
sun breaks into two red circles upon the
                    carried frothing—
white and roiling, yes, yet unbreakably red—red pushed (slicked) under
                    each wave (tucked) and, although breaking, always
                    one—(as if from the back-end-of-distance red)—
and that *one* flowing to here to
slap the red it carries in glisten-sheets
up onto shore and (also as if *onto*)
my feet.

*

[Or onto my feet, then into my eyes] where red turns into "sun" again.
So then it's sun in surf-breaking water: incircling, smearing: mind not
knowing if it's still "wave," breaking on
itself, small glider, or if it's "amidst" (red turning feathery)
or rather "over" (the laciness of foambreak) or just *what*—(among

the line of also smearingly reddening terns floating out now
on the feathery backedge of foambroken
looking)—*it is.*

*

The wind swallows my words one
by
one. The words leaping too, over their own
staying.
Oceanward too, as if being taken
away
into splash—my clutch of
words
swaying and stemming from my
saying, no
echo. No stopping on the temporarily exposed and drying rock
out there
to rub or rest where nothing else
grows.
And truly swift over the sands.
As if most afraid of being re-
peated.
Preferring to be dissolved to
designation,
backglancing stirrings,
wedged-in between unsaying and
forgetting—
what an enterprise—spoken out by
me as if

to *still* some last place, place becoming even as I speak

                      unspeakable—

and so punctually—not even burnt

by their crossing through the one great

               inwardness of

mind, not by the straining to be held (grasped) by my

                   meanings:

"We shall have early fruit

this year" one of the shades along the way

            calls out,

and "from the beginning" (yet further on). Words: always face-down:

listening falling upon them (as if from

              above):

listening greedy, able to put them to death,

flinging itself upon them: them open and attached

          so hard to

           what they carry:

the only evidence in them of having

           been.

And yet how they want to see behind themselves—

         as if there is something

back there, always, behind these rows I

      gnaw the open with—

feeling them rush a bit and crane to see beneath themselves—

and always with such pain, just after emerging—

twisting on their stems to see behind—as if there were a

               sun

back there they need, as if it's a betrayal,

this single forward-facing: reference: dream of: ad-

           mission: re

semblance: turning away from the page as if turning to a tryst:

the gazing-straight up at the reader there filled with ultimate

fatigue:

devoted servants: road signs: footprints: you are not alone:

slowly in the listener the prisoners emerge:

slowly in you reader they stand like madmen facing into the wind:

nowhere is there any trace of blood

spilled in the service of kings, or love, or for the sake of honor,

or for some other reason.

DUSK SHORE PRAYER

The creeping revelation of shoreline.

The under-shadowed paisleys scripting wave-edge down-

slope

on the barest inclination, sun making of each

milelong wave-retreat

a golden translucent forward downgoing,

golden sentences writ on clearest moving waters,

moving their meaninglessness on (not *in*) the moving of the

waters

(which feels tugged)(the rows of scripting

[even though it's a trick] adamant with

self-unfolding)(wanting the eye to catch and take

dominant final-hold, feel the thickest rope of

waterlipped

scripting

to be a producing of a thing that speaks [to whom

one does not know, but a true speech])—to believe this truly,

not in metaphor—

to put it in the blank in which one *sees,*

and then into the blank in which one *is,*

to separate *I am* from *I have being* from *I am*

apart. And not to want to *be*. And never to be

emptied by the wound of meaning.

The gash of likeness. The stump interpretation.

Spelled from the living world. Grown sharper by

this sighting. As sun goes down. Until it glimmers in

the tiny darkness and the human will comes to the end.
Having it go before one's looking goes. The summer
at one's back. The path back barely findable.

THE COMPLEX MECHANISM OF THE BREAK

From here, ten to fourteen rows of folding and branching.

Up close, the laving in overlappings that pool sideways as well as suck back.

Filamentary green-trims where the temporary furthest

                    coming-forward is lost.

Suctions in three or four different directions back from pinnacle-point.

Encounter of back-suck by the foremost,

                low-breaking, upstitching really,

arrivals,

      where it seems pebblings of sandbits ruffle-up and are ruffled

                      back into the foam of

                    the breakwater browning it.

Glassy meanwhile the frontmost arrivals, their sheets filling momentarily with

sky,with clouds fully formed (in which gulls [of sand] glide) even as they all

                          are drawn back

into the ruffling front-thunder

into which direct backmotion

feeds—is fed—(over which real rows of low-flying pelicans)—

(backmotion into which retreat itself feeds, slides, you'd have to say dissolves)—

(though strangely nothing of the sea dissolves).

Behind: the crystalline green risings of just-before furling,

then the furling. Between: the wild-carrot lacings and

                  spume of

breakages the eye hardly caught. Lifting the eyes away one sees

in the near/far distance large upwallings

in which sometimes fish calmly ride sideways

              above one,

high above, while close-up, the sky unfolds, deep, here, at our

                                    feet—

(the eyes look down to see up)—(then, squinting, out, to see

                    the see-through slow uprising

                    holding its school). The mind doesn't

want it to break—unease where the heart pushes out—the mind

wants only to keep it coming, yes, sun making the not-yet-breaking crest

                                    so gold where the

pelicans turn as they glide—flapping then gliding—

as long as possible without too much dropping—

here and there trying to stay with the just-breaking ridge,

turning towards or away from the

                    watching-eye

to origami trick, artichoke wing—sheen—crank—beaks dragging the

gold-fringed, gathered garment-furl through which

                    the fish themselves drive (thread)

the only momentarily unbreaking line. And how there is always something

else. Up close four different brown retreating furls just now (being forced

                                    to forward-break) re-

entering themselves. Each tripping over each as they are also forced

                                    into retreat.

What is force? My love is forced from me as in retreat

from love. My gaze is forced back into me as it retreats

from thought. Sometimes the whole unraveling activity

                    for just an instant

pools, all its opposing motions suddenly just pattern on these briefly

lakelike flats—the shore's upslant unspooling then in only two

                    dimensions—(close your eyes)—

(although it's only when you open them you hear the seven

                                    kinds of

sound: hiss-flattenings and poolings-out [sand-suctions in the
flat],
the pebbled wordlike pulling down and rolling up, the small
hush of the small first-line of white, it lowering its
voice as it proceeds
to crash, the crash where the larger one behind is hit and hits
the one of yet more force
behind it now, the singleness—[the one loud
thunder-break]—the backmost individual wave,
the lowering and sudden softening of all betweens [of which
every few minutes one] out of which the first crash
yet again can rise. Also the momentary lull: which now lets in
the sound of distance in itself: where your eye might
look up, further out: to where, it seems,
nothing but steady forward progress in its perfect
time occurs: onward, onward: tiny patterns which
seen from above must: it is imagined: perfectly: shine).

EBBTIDE

I am a frequency, current flies through. One has

         to ride

         the spine.

No peace [of mind][of heart], among the other

frequencies. How often and how hard are answerings.

The surf, receding, leaves successive

hem-line trims of barely raised institching sand—

bridal-wreath puckerings—

glassy (this side), packed smooth (that).

Making one's way one sees the changes.

What took place before one

         looked.

Snakeskin of darker sands in with the light.

Slightly more raised and wider alligator-skins.

Crabtracks' wild unfocusings around firm holes.

The single tubefish, dead, long as a snake, half-snout,

rolled over and over as the waves pick up, return, return

less often, go away. For a while he is incandescent

white, then blue, deep green, then white again, until he's

         left, half-turned,

eyes sandy till one wave, come back

this far as if in error, cleans him off.

Greenish with rising/falling weed-debris, shoremist

fingering long streaks of sun.

Graphed beachlength on the scallop-edged lapping retreat:

         christmas-ornament red shrimp

punctually along the highs of each

upskirting arc—prongs upright,

stiff. Swift ticks of sunlight count them

                                      out.

Who has enough? A little distance

                          back

two vultures feeding on a pelican. Later, claws and beak

float in the brack. Foam-bits lace-up the edge

of the retreat. Something feels like it's not

coming back. In the tidepool

sand-grains advance along a long

walled avenue, in ranks—at the conjunction of

                          two rocks, algae

signaling the entry point—(swarming but

                          swaying in

unison, without advancing) (waiting for

                          some arrival)

(the channel of them quickening)(the large espousal)(light

beginning now to *touch* what had been only

                          underwater story)—

until the gleaming flow of particles is finally

                          set down, is

                          stilled: the grains

drop down and mat, silt in, begin to dry: the wandering tribe is

                          gone, the

city's gone, the waiting gone. The individual grains

are not discernible. I'm squatting so I hear

sand sucking water in. Gravity. Glistening.

I take a stick and run it through

the corridor of wilderness.

It fills a bit with water the first time. Is self-erased.

The second time it does not fill. It leaves a

                          mark where

my stick ran. I make

another (cursive) mark. How easily it bends to cursive, snakes towards

thought.

Looking back

I see the birds eating the bird. The other way my

gaze can barely reach shore-break.

The (little) weight of the stick in my hand. The meditation

place demands. My frequency. This hand, this

sugar-stalk. The cane-fields in the back of us,

the length of tubefish back there too. And

if I write my name. And how mist rounds the headland

till the sea

is gone. One feels word should be sent us

from some source. It is all

roar and cry and suck and snap. The pebbles on the

pebbles roll. One feels one has in custody

what one cannot care for for long. Too much is

asked. Nothing is coming back the way it was.

But one can wait for the next hem, next bride,

next oscillation, comedy. Done, the birds fly

off. I can see through the trees,

through the cane grove, palm grove, out far enough into

the clearing where

the spine of the picked-clean story shines.

HUNGER

(Midday)

"As if twelve princes sat before a king" (Wallace Stevens)

11:54

Thirteen fullest oranges pooling at the foot of
                                                their tree.
In the crater carved-out to contain water at
                                        watering.
Rolled down, touching each other, gleaming.
At watering: heard the early morning
                        hiss (and deeper
                        lengthenings)—right in the
                        birdsound—sometimes
                        cutting all the way through
                        as pouring-
                        forth got
closer. Also heard
the soil in the cool taking the water
in—but can't tell
how to card it [hear it]
            out. Now
the eight-foot yucca on its almost-straight
                        peeling-back
                        stalk
casting a "perfect" sharp black crown [also halo] on the
                        ground: right
                        at its own

[*39*]

foot—so that it grows out of its own reflection—or, no,

out of the reflection of

its blossom-head—the stalk [not

visible in shadow] packed wholly into the eye of the

ground-crown out of which

the actual stem

starts up to *cause*. The cause

(of the crown): yucca leaves

(now in the third dimensional)

traveling out in all the directions, holding the watery sunlight

most in the deepest nesting

center-driven parts of each

individual leaf, but in the widest cases traveling all

the way up to the tip

making white-yellow interlacings of sunbearing fronds twine-up with

utterly darkened ones:

the undersides almost black: me now looking down to see

the crown in its

second dimension (shadow)

move: boy

dragging a bucket at middle distance:

weight in its drag:

me watching the actual crown move in its third.

11:57

Wind-motion: yucca leaves: *shape* moving identically

in both dimensions: wind-motion

only damaging the narrative—(color, relation,

field-to-ground)—in the actual:

the *shadowed* moves with—is—sun—time:

the *actual* told time and time again by sun, a

story, no illusion: a sheet being flapped out

just to the left: behind a

thatched wall: a woman's voice in the sheet—

then snapping—[to shake a dry thing out]—smell of midday in the sheet—[to fold

a dry thing up]—

then song turning to string of words, rising pitch,

11:58

hands gripping, snapping, and so forth (in the invisible):

high laughter—quick—where words,

rushed out like shadow of the song, elicit

11:59

response: then two at once: drone of inevitable unfolding; exfoliating

highs of

11:59

response: above the orange tree's full head of fruit, one

largest-of-all-palms swaying lazily

right through the strongest wind-bursts—

12:00

Everything moving away from core

All patterning being motion-away-from-origin

The limited number of directions a thing can go in

The buzzard above, the furrows of *its* feathers

The circling

Where what one can't look straight-up-at is

Where the yellow hose crossing the dirt yard
makes its circular loop (no shadow)

Where my eye picks it up just as the silence breaks

Where I count six kinds of leaf

hushing and slurring—an engine nearing then
re-disappearing—

[the king down to the one-body-under-the-sun moves, a
caw in the leaf-hissings making itself their core, also
drawing onto them a scale of
relative darkenings, hierarchy hearable as a
drawing of likeness towards its own register, the
blackness of the crow nowhere visible yet fisting
the core].

12:01

The loop in the yellow then the
yellow continuing.

12:01

All the fruit darkening.

12:01

A child whining.

A path when I get to it. The having-moved. The given.

The given sun. The befallen. Why is it the thief gets into heaven.

In this description the layer of thieving.

In all the leaves geometry so adamant.

As if in enough heat the mind is forced inside to

watch: to feel: fear: geometry: rot: math:
light.

(later)

The god: repetition without variant:
its spouse: inevitable necessary variant: its lover: unnecessary
variant: interruption, wall, disease, rot.

(later)

Inevitable

Inanimate

(later)

What can be broken always holding what can [not].
A truth not a symbol. Grip it in scrutiny.

THE TIME BEING

I
(Todos Santos)

Cluster of bird-chatter a knot at the center of a supreme
unfolding. Large river-pebbles almost filling a jar.
Turn it over: where they collide and recollect: that grainy quick
clatterfall: cluster: [of birdsound]: knot.

Near it a browner sound, closer-up, a
single note of it a very thick rope, stiff with age, knotted
to a rusted hinge: in it a higher and a lower pitch (inter-
                              mingling)
(rope squeak and hinge). But that only if the one note (repeated
more or less rapidly)(in clusters of up to five) is singled
out.

Nothing can be singled out.

*

We wait for the dog-bark, hearing sun (utterly without
glow in it)(a thing that blanks out into what we call
blindness each thing it washes) in the highest background
lymph-system screeches. Clap of banana leaves, long as a
tall child or marlin. Then the dog-bark to the
far left—for a moment just *itself,*
then the dog-bark drawn in, percussive, in
relation. Then we wait for the first car.

*

Engine rising [we know there's a hill] then evening-out to a

smooth hum, then into the story with fictive

presence, even as it crosses through the length of town then out.

When the woman calls out, it's not as if the netting

caught her. She knots up the far left of

the listening. A small boy suddenly very near to the

right taps a glass jar with a metal

implement, then he taps a different openness.

*

The listening: one is the first of

the fishermen. The net builds. It casts

still further. The trucks on the highway passing town. The

goatbells and cowbells intermingling at the edge of the

canefields. One is first first. Then there is a

portal, saints pass through, light

over all of it without nearing, but shadows

striating our shadows' passing-in, adding-through.

One is first then one is suddenly unable to be

first, it is a strange quick grace. The net

shifts hands, is held at the other side, at the

far side (churchbell for 17 repeats like lower

goatbell)(all sounds always reproducible

[if one rejects name] as something damaged or

frayed or about to break

from wear). One feels sound deepest in the apparently

most worn. In this sunlight, for

instance. Here. Just as I say this and the

chatter rises in a clump I know not in

response to what. Just here where the

sunlight crosses my sill and the

window-sashes lay firm gray-black marks

aslant the terracotta tiles of floor. Here

where the whiteness of the "vacancy" the palmfronds (full of

transparency and motion) carry back and forth over floortiles' grout-lines—here

where that whitening (wind really) juts wild through

$$\text{all strands of}$$

the netting (sash, grout, palmfrond) and is, of a sudden, made to let up, slow

$$\text{down, as the}$$

caught fish must.

II

(Palm Beach, Todos Santos)

The whole of the unfolding like a skin

coming-off. Sand striated everywhere by tide-action

packed hard onto it in tiny color variations and

speckling and runs of diamond-pattern where tide

has receded. Monkfish with their porcupine-quilled

tapering backs, all head and side-eyes and quickly

left by the tides. At tide-line, with each

lapping, shrimp left at the greenish fanning wave

$$\text{edge.}$$

Retreat and more retreat. Tiretracks

recriss-crossing the marbled sandskin. Footprints,

birdprints, feathers, broken glass. The fishermen

in the distance on the rocks casting out.

Wallbreaks, the filament where the backwash

breaks and retreats leaving a pooling, white and green,

and also brownish marbled slicknesses [a tiny

stilling, really, in the regrouping of powers] and on

that slickness: filmy slownesses like lung

tissue, or the white netting from

stomach-lining they wrap lamb-kidneys in in the window

display—slightly fatty and good in baking where it

holds the parts together then melts off—

Here melting off: the skin of the

momentary lull where forward and backward

motion are ever so briefly equal—feathery too [so soft] but

mostly marbled [so hard]

yet sloughing snakeskin off with the very next

wave and laying that skin onto shore, at

our feet. In sand: on sand:

palmfronds, feather-layerings: accumulations of differently-gapped nets at

angles not exactly overlapping: drifts of

miniscule dune-structures building like sound-waves

then lowering in sun in fast-moving clouds: making

for the time being, the time being: tide coming back

in and the fishermen now walking this way carrying off

an unusually large catch. The

story that got me here. The breaking waves tossing

spume the whole length of the beach. The glassy

tidal-retreat zone where the reduced

incline allows for a full measure of sky

every eight seconds or so to be strewn over the

otherwise dark-wet sand—a sun, a blueness,

clouds clearly moving, the skin of water

giving us "where-the-earth-opens" [it must open],

sun in there one cannot look at any

more than one can look at the one above—then the retreat—

sun, clouds, blue, all being taken back

into the shorebreak, tossed-up, in-ruffled

airily into huge plumes and upcast mists, the looking-down

leaving tiny holes where clam and crab and tubeworm

suck back under and the water goes *down* as well as *out*

and the earth is filling and the earth is

shut. The time presses.

The sense of one's *person*

numbs as in having been too long in too

strong a wind. The idea won't

hold as I push it out. Then it will. Then it

is held [not by me]. Then it is all gone.

The fishermen seen from the back as they

disappear through the palms.

III

PRAYER
("From Behind Trees")

The branchful of dried leaves blown about at the center

of the road, turning on itself is it a path:

snake: gray-brown updrafting: drama:

whole affair played out between the wind's quiver, wind's

dusty haste, an almost impeccable procedure,

bit of scenery from which all fear

is deleted. So it

is right here, where I am peering, where I am supposed to

discern,

how the new gods walk behind the old gods at the suitable distance.

EXIT WOUND

The apparently sudden appearance of—

                  blossoming-out afresh, out of reach—

aiming for extinction, abandonment—

                  other fossils, then again no fossils—

because of having previously lived on earth,

deviating and branching into use and disuse,

what in it that is transmitted by heredity,

that cannot help the lowest plants and animals—

what is "the lowest," where ends "environment,"

"he was therefore unable to provide a unitary theory of

                      evolution,"

to use reason to arrive at faith,

to bring the sacred into the branchings of the un-

reasonable—the blue between the branches

pulling upwards and away so that branches

                become

branching, their tips failing at what comes to be called dis-

                  appearance,

as if by too much compromise, straining towards justice till it

                  cannot but

fail. Alongside faith (leaping) always the

            demon, the

comparative. The presence [only the mind can do

            this] of

inner feeling up against *living force*,

what exists without having been perfected or made

            complex,

what exists without having been made,

what exists without having been,

(therefore unable to provide a unitary theory)

(of evolution)(of regret)

what exists inside the sensation of duration—

(inside duration where is the aside to go)(how

far under)(or is it into?)—and then in the aside, the off-

hand, half-formulated, half-heard but yet still

                  living breath of a

thinking, down in the deep station of feeling—

          though still (barely) out-

lined so as to be [branching] as-

         certainable

and seizable, so as to be dragged up: there, she

                thought,

is my thought before me. Like a planted

thing in its pot. Not quite in nature

         yet still alive

and—most crucially—self-evident.

And that I can feed it. [Yet she was unable still

to provide a unitary theory]. It is

(she thought looking away momentarily)(so that

looking back it could be there more fully in all

its glory: her thought) however small, a

          catastrophe,

leafing and branching, making of itself a higher

            and a lower

part, catastrophic, down to its

shadows cast upon the floor,

branchings so still where the leaf-ends

          sway

in the breeze the curtains have

touched and left off.

Outside, she thought: the point of origin.

They can call it, if they wish, she thought, the

                             supreme

being (blossoming-out afresh)(feeling as if one

had previously lived elsewhere on earth)

(out of reach even of catastrophe)(there had been,

she knew, extensive extinctions) her

                  thinking this now

deep in the *duration* [wanting

so to come back up][but up into what

               organism of

time][or is it organization of?] the *lasting* of the minutes

                    for example,

the sensation of their being somewhere clocked

                  out in a re-

sistant form, a wage for example attached to

their beginnings and endings, beginnings and endings

                somehow capable of being

               exactly

cut off. That not catastrophic, therefore, for

               example.

Not the organism of catastrophe like a

shaft of light breaking down through the crowning trees

just now [*in* the just now] as she looked out.

And could she be *associated* with it, for example,

               that instant

of looking-up and light breaking through, could she

be imbricated into the fate [the fate's non-

               durational

nature for example][even the recess in which
these "for examples" go][always in it, all
$$\text{levels of}$$
$$\text{inwardness}—$$
the progress by the abandonment
of some aspects of creation
$$\text{to fate]}$$
[we call this progressionism][but there is
also the correlation of parts][in order
to determine the space to which we, each,
belong][or could it be felt—or thought—
that everything happening now was strictly
connected to something that *happened* in
the past][it was the word "happened" stopped her]
the problem as always was the problem of how
something could come out of nothing.
There was no other question: inside her,
the nothing [she could just feel it] and before her,
[the plant on the table] the something, the thought
of the nothing [for example]. The Creator loomed
$$\text{(as it always happens)}$$
outside, a bit far away, but still filling-in for
the unexpected. She heard the kitchen clock's gears and also the noon
$$\text{churchbells}$$
on the far hill. She thought of the idea
$$\text{of happiness}$$
—where to place that—like a string of
$$\text{christmas lights}$$
dropping down into a darkened well
$$\text{or tomb [or was it}$$

catacomb]. She saw the images flash on

and off

according to the swinging of the lights. *Down there*

she thought. She thought

of happiness, the principal part of the

thinking of the thing,

its highest part, still reachable from up here by the

mind, she thought, as though a pronounced

looking-down,

vertiginous, a squinting, yes, but as if

one species of one's self could look back

far enough

(although of course here it was *down*) to

see the previous existent one had been—

the mark of *design* there upon the gap

between them now (the christmas lights)

(the swaying intermittence of)

(the hiddenness between the frequencies)

(the frequencies)—She felt as if she could

reconcile

this present to that one, and that the

thinking

wanted that so. And that it strived.

EVOLUTION

One's nakedness is very slow.

One calls to it, one wastes one's sympathy.

Comparison, too, is very slow.

Where is the past?

I sense that we should keep this coming.

Something like joy rivulets along the sand.

I insists that we "go in." We go in.

One cannot keep all of it. What is enough

of it. And *keep?*—I am being swept away—

what is *keep?* A waking good.

Visibility blocking the view.

Although we associate the manifest with kindness.

The way it goes where it goes, slight downslope.

Like the word "suddenly," the incline it causes.

Also the eye's wild joy sucked down the slope the minutes wave

                                        by wave

pack down and slick.

The journey—some journey—visits one.

The journey—some journey—visits me.

Then this downslope once again.

And how it makes what happens

        always more heavily

laden, this self only able to sink (albeit also lifting

                        as in a

sudden draught) into the future. *Our* future. Where everyone

is patient. Where all the sentences come to complete themselves.

Where what wants to be human still won't show

                        its face.

ESTUARY

She wondered about the year 1000. She
worried the long stretch of horizon's
         yellow gapping of
sea from sky with an uplifted glance. She
worried its fixity till it wasn't fixed. She
felt the calling herself *she* as the exact
spot she closed her eyes and the whole un-
           spooled—miles,
beach, mist, spray, outcroppings, current-drawn
nettings of foam that fanned-out in lulls
as if to give the sea a top—oh please—a
resistant stillness on which to scroll—a
flat impenetrability windowlike out onto a
dark that allows only for this reflection,
this side's insistence, to lay itself upon the
glancing pane: foaming scripts, eyes that
follow and follow frantic with indirection. What
is history to this instant between the waves
[she let herself think][although she was really
thinking let me think, let me just think it and it
will still and come forth][and there will be,
         however invisible to
others, an annunciation][she
put it there again, as if onto the flat foamy
widening between waves, right onto its
hush, the year 1000]. She felt it was a test.
All of this. She heard it hard, that word, *this.*
It seemed to furl-out as from an opening,

a gesture of mind geometric in its widening,

so firm, the this of the visible

and of nothing else. None of the *thinking* she so laid

down hard, the gesture that of the practiced

plasterer spreading the thin gesso

on the church wall, early morning, circa 1000

flat and clean this one arc of his firm

trowel. Now it, the arc, at each degree of its wide math,

can leave the bodies of sleeping saints and move

across the heaven of

the in-front (and sometimes-a-bit-above) visible.

How odd it all is. Was it better when we were

sure, losers of the big game and sure, vision on our heads like

helmets, gleaming, moving downriver, slowly

but surely, excavating new metals as we

went, opening new trees, crafting new weapons of

highest beauty [we were after gold][also of course

in search of slaves][where are they?][also victory]

[what we call saleable value][thirsty] and yet

what is she now that the rimmed gap

between water and sky is empurpling [lay me down

at my lord's right hand][though I am white with

listening (looking) I will not away][lay me

down by my lord's right hand][we are

bloodthirsty, but after legend][after easily

removable booty] strong with gods' consent

[also from our forefathers]. Payment is required.

As I look out [dusk lowering the *she* as well, down,

onto the horizon line, then drawing in, towards singleness, pulling in,

as nets must be pulled in]—so she

looks out, becoming *I*, feeling it to be a

test, counting the lowering pelican squadron

as it rides the goldening crest of one wave, banking

this side then that of it, dipping as low as breaking

allows, fantastic touching-down behind the break, not un-

predictable except by me [and some of us]

[not you]["lord you," but that is love][that

beseeching sound in the core of the self]

also the frigate birds who bank their black and sheer

white scissoring tails [dowsing for wind in

                                    priestly strictness]

twelve circling in a cantata now, then a variation left and

right to reconverge [sometimes as raiders

coming upriver for nubile girls or even wives]

[their thanes forced to look on] then banked at the edge of

human peripheral vision, then circling back

above the fishing spot, the break, and just

behind the break, the lull (how can I say

how much is in the lull)[in pursuit of][casual booty]

[casual beauty][(who) had territorial ambitions

carrying downriver towards this mouthing]

[whose value the king could easily

appreciate][song] the notes of the inaudible frigate fugue

regrouping to the gorgeous asymmetries of center,

a prosperity—even duples and triplets in their

line-up, strong-stress and then liquefaction—

a large sum of money being counted

and recounted, a sum being paid in tribute, out of

fear, being recounted again (they part,

grow single, drop, regroup) out of fear,

gold, the watching eye never able to count out

the tribute, unable to get its defense organized,
[everyone on the beach now waiting for the fishing boats]
[what there is is readiness and
waiting][and chance][earlier, near noon, the
man and his son sleeping in the slim shadow the
                              boat casts on
the sand, nestled up against
the blue stripe of boat-bottom, keel,
stray asleep in another pool, ticking of
trucks cooling down—morning-sale long gone—called-out
                              prices—
thrift, need, quickness]
also the-trying-every-angle (from the instant the
                    small-craft touch down)
also dogs lapping, pelicans, seagulls, frigates, one
                    sea lion. She
looked into the dark. I, I. She tried every angle
[the solution to the invader's debilitation
was to try to buy off the raiders]["protection"]
["money"][paying them to go away][gold]
[unearthed by modern archeologists][modern]
am asked to look [she has slimmed so] to where
I cannot quite much longer see. Am asked. By
what. The god now total conquest. Loyalty. We are
where the river spills and sea is all.

KYOTO

Commentary continues, slanting downward.

Ah what am I carrying, what's this load, who's that

out there,

why all this dust? I remember "the oldest of trees."

We drove through it. I "looked." I remember

"all manner of being may swim in my sea."

Slanting upward, tiny bits of rain murmur in my gaze.

Slanting upward, the gaze senses, right *in* the looking—[so

fresh][after

rain, early spring]—the gaze cannot but sense [since

it's not in the

visual field][not at all]—cannot but: the slantline down towards

dis-

appearance. Remember:

the statues you were looking at [in the

old world] row after row in the beautiful garden,

veined-marble after spring rain (so-called), weight placed on the one

leg or the other, as if in gravity, although also actually

in gravity,

arm on a hip, arm holding a

book, a sword, a severed head—a bow, stone quills—some grapes

proferred, long gazing out, long avenues of principles, adorned, with self,

with

representation, naked for the most part, trees just-in-leaf all down

the lanes,

and everywhere *principle*, hidden but manifest, what we have made

link up in the

spine of time [the body of human making]—right there along with the

million grasses waving [in the new world] right there—aspen visible

at medium height on the near slope, just budding out—

ah what am I carrying, what is this on the ground—

or the ocean lying on its side

whispering—or the silkworm-mulberry, the damasks and brocades covering the

globe,

the hush of sateen-foldings over stone, the hiss in the human walk,

in palaces, in dancehalls—or vineyards sloping away near hilltop—

or look down on sea-top, you'll see wind-design—yes—from

here—

[where are we][who's that in the dust?][is there sleeping

anymore]

["whispering": will it always exist]["mirroring": will it always

exist]

[breath on the mirror if you should get so close]

priorities, humilities, imitation, dew-drenching, intellectuality,

[meet near the resting-place][the white-rose wall][equal to][un

equal

to]—so that if [uneasiness in the face of sunset][uneasiness in the face

of sunrise] I ask you now [with unexpected ease]

[with rapid extension of mind, leaping] to come back from

here

to the statues lining the avenue [mind/gaze now darting down it with

a strange foraging hope][as if feeding very quickly and furiously],

ask you to see them blow up: to dust: all "at once": or "one at a time":

down the wide avenue: lining both sides: dawn slowly creeping toward the rim of

visibility: something maybe observing this: from somewhere: the air

soft, warm, known to the bluebird and swallow: then ask you to

rewind [for just][two seconds]

and see [even eyes closed] see this: wings touching then overlapping
each other slowly as the landed bird re-

      settles. This
I was thinking today: all you can know: then plants and
animals: names of: movements of: your love: your hands: of
when I was ten in Kyoto mother insisting I take
flower-arranging classes: every morning in a city building:
white stone! with many steps up: then a vast room:
acidy smell of fresh-cuttings, thousands: oozing stem-ends:
eyes: hundreds of greens: and
perfumes: and shinings of movement where two hands lift
       stem-ends:
and color-flash through air to angled-anchorings: said to reveal the
      truth of *us*: the
four elements: "represented": the harmonies: to give a state of
mind [not pleasure][what is pleasure] what is she
carrying the young woman still bringing the still-wet branches of blossom in
through the small door to the left under her arms: almond and
cherry: changes: not dream not at all that
would be disappearance: who rules this:
more brought in every day: the birds of the finished
    (your eye's flight around it). See,
you have picked many flowers. You will pick many more.
As for instance in this "thinking" "today" [two blossomheads
there]. There will be flowers forever. This is: Spring, today, April, 2001.
This I am carrying. These branchings, these cuttings. With a whole heart.

The questions:
   What is longest? oldest? truest? plenty?
   Wisdom? Peace? Wavering? Misfortune?

The rules:

> One must be blameless.
>
> One must come to loneliness and be lonely.
>
> One must know half from whole.
>
> One must hear the "broken carriage springs" and know them for
>> the cowbird's unoiled-gate-hinge
>
> song. Nothing is partial. One must know partiality.
>
> She picks it up and puts it down again.
>
> One must see the cowbird spread its tail—just so—and
>> shut it again, clean, just
>
> after landing. One must know. The rut is the carriage-trail.
>
> Which carriage. The passage through trees—which bird. When.
>
> Feeble sounds. Harsh. Missed perchings. Repetition: its
>
> insistent coolness: me me me me says one bird, nameless,
>
> who has heard what is dead. It's invisible. It must be heard
>> of.

Invisible bouquet:

> [a generation ago][the forests
>
> were][I assemble my books][we plan to]
>
> [formerly][assume the posture][of]
>
> [rushing]   [just a moment ago]
>
>   [suddenly]
>
>   [breathless with excitement she]
>
>   [best not to]
>
>   [is different now]
>
>   [crown the color of]
>
> [hearing the wild birds in their]
>
>   [although it's early morning, I]
>
> [dark forelock combed back, damp]
>
>   [days]

SOLITUDE

*

The subject of mutability
Fog   hour   tree   (frogs)
(mourning dove/hiss of train uncoupling)
(inaudible component to operatic sunset)

*

The subject of mutability
Graduation that can be imagined
Graduation that cannot be imagined
(Difference)   (Series)
Appearance out of nowhere of the new
Life-history   Monstrous birth

*

Need that provokes satisfaction of that need.
Account for origin of [such and such]
Change   Undergone
Lust   Hunger   Danger
Cross-fertilize   Maintain vigor
          [protective]
of the significance   of the vestigial
presupposes   a former function
the power of acquiring new parts
attended by new propensities
directed by irritations sensations volitions associations

*

Editor: their possessing the power to continue [to improve?]

        by their own inherent activity,

        delivering those improvements to posterity——?

*

Speaking subject: world without end

*

Animal   Kingdom

Branching   Limbs

(The last branch the branch I'm on)

(The final branching)

*

Had not become extinct

Had been transmuted into living

*

The supposed tendency to perfection

The supposed tendency to increased complexity

The supposed scale of being

The supposed bottom the supposed top

*

ed: allusion to another work

s.s: I do not hold before me the words

    I do not hold before me the words said and under

    stood.

ed: perceiving subject speaking subject thinking subject

s.s: I have to trace a path

    I am sinking into the local the temporal open,

    that other-than-me who is the I

ed: I said: the openness to the world such as we re-

    discover it in ourselves and the perception within life

    intertwine, encroach upon, change to one another

s.s: consciousness seeking to see time and not to measure it

s.s: consciousness that is at once spontaneous and reflected

        [on the same page]

        the look that kills

[my "look"]   [the presence of what is behind my back]

    (self-presence which is not *an absence from oneself*)

        (the figure on the ground)

(it is already the flesh of things that speaks to us of our own

    flesh, and that speaks to us of the flesh of the other)

                    *

you must rise   it is said

by anomaly   deviation   branching

from what might have been

the environment interfered

the environment interferes

new needs because of inner feeling

internal   feeling

living   force

out of catastrophe blooms afresh

                    *

also extensive   extinction

a new concept of love involving abandonment

creation (of melancholy fate) by supreme being

*

After catastrophe   advance in the complexity
    of superiority   of purpose

*

of the effects   of internal sentiment
of the effects of acts of obliteration
look back   become
[not magnification]   [but change]

*

reformation   realization

*

a part taken away

*

no whole

*

the idea of development enters the world

*

Such is the machinery of perfection: loss
Such is the machinery of history: habit
Such is the sacred theology: history
Trace continuity through recapitulation
Not magnification, but change

*

The eye is adapted to the medium in which
it lives: agency, wisdom, progression, anticipation.
So the idea of development enters into
the world.

*

s.s: Let us therefore consider ourselves installed
among the multitude of things. Let us try to form notions
that would enable us to comprehend what happens
to us there. Our first truth—which prejudges
nothing and cannot be contested—will be that
there is

ed: one is tempted to say, "the things"—

s.s: presence, that "something" is there, and that "someone"
is there. Before coming to the "someone," let us ask first

ed: one is tempted to say "the things"…
Everyone knows apparently what must be

s.s: what the "something" is.

ed: understood by that?

IV

COVENANT

This in an age in which imagination

is no longer all-powerful. Where if you had

to write the whole thing down, you could.

(Imagine: to see the whole thing written down).

Everything but memory abolished.

All the necessary explanations also provided.

A very round place: everyone is doing it.

"It": a *very* round and glad place.

Feeling life come from far way, like a motor approaching.

And in its approach: that moment when it is closest, so loud, as if

not only near you, but *in* you.

And *that* being the place where the sensation of real property

begins. Come. It is going to pass, even though right

now

it's very loud, here, alongside, life, life, so glad to be in it,

no?, unprotected, thank you, *exactly* the way I feel.

And you? Lord how close it comes. It has a

seeming to it

so bright it is as if it had no core.

It all given over to the outline of seem:

still approaching, blind, open, its continuing *elsewhere* unthinkable as a

gear-shift

at this speed.

Approaching as if with a big question.

No other system but this one and it growing larger.

All at once, as if all the voices now are suddenly one voice.

Ah, it is here now, *the here*. [Love, where is love, can it too be this thing that simply grows insistently louder]

[It seems impossible it could ever pass *by*][she thought]

this eruption of presentness right here: your veins

[Meanwhile a dream floats in an unvisited field]

[There by the edge of the barn, above the two green-lichened

stones, where for an instant a butterfly color of chicory

                                flicks, dis-

appears]. How old fashioned: distance: squinting it

                              into

view. Even further: rocks at year's lowest tide.

The always-underneath excitedly exposed to heat, light, wind, the

being-seen. Who could have known a glance could be

so plastic. Rubbery and pushing-down on all the tiny hissing overbright

                                        greens.

O sweet conversation: protozoa, air: how long have you been speaking?

The engine [of *the most*] is passing *us* now.

At peak: the mesmerization of here, this me here, this me

passing now.

So as to leave *what* behind?

We, who can now be neither wholly here nor disappear?

And to have it come so close and yet not *know* it:

how in time you do *not* move on:

how there is no "other" side:

how the instant is very wide and bright and we cannot

                              ever

get away with it—the instant—what holds the "know"

[as if gently, friend, as if mesmerized by love of *it*][love of

(not) making sense](tide coming in)(then distance taking

                          the complexion

                          of engine

whitely in)(the covenant, the listening, drawing its parameters out

just as it approaches its own unraveling)

the covenant: yes: that there be plenitude, yes,

but only as a simultaneous emptying—of the before, where it came

from—and of the after (the eager place to which it so

"eagerly" goes). Such rigorous logic, that undulating shape

                              we make of

                              our listening

to it: being: being on time: in time: there seeming to be no actual

                                        being:

all of it growing for a time closer and closer—as with a freight

                              of sheer abstract

                              abundance (the motor

sound)(is all) followed by the full selfishness (of such

                    well being) of the being

(so full of innocence) actually (for the instant) here:

I love you: the sky seems nearer: you are my first

                    person:

let no one question this tirelessness of approach:

love big enough to hide the cage:

tell them yourself who you are:

no victory: ever: no *ever*: then what "happens":

you can hear the hum at its most constant: famished: the era:

          love bestowed upon love close-up:

(quick, ask it of heaven now, whatever it was you so

                    wished to

know) the knowing: so final: yet here is the road, the

                    context, ongoingness,

and how it does go on regardless of the strangely sudden coming un-

                              done of

its passing away.

Silence is welcomed without enthusiasm.

Listening standing now like one who removed his hat

out of respect for

the passage.

What comes in the aftermath they tell us is richly

satisfying.

No need to make a story up, for instance.

We have been free now ever since, for instance.

WHERE: THE PERSON

The background, as the car with its music begins

to recede, first reasserting itself through an increasingly un-

               differentiated

tick and boom—the baseline's disappearance like one you once loved, one

still waving, you squinting, trying to both see *and* remember—

an urge once "everything" subduing now, down to small-talk, a little chat,

dried flowers staring from a shiny bowl—

then, all round them, increasing: "considerable" distance: the sense of a stranger now

                               off to

some other business—him *too* now waving—his back the only part you

understand, a stranger's back, receding, of

a certain size, yes, a semi-darkening object, an object of

attention, human. Oh lord what is it. A tent-flap falls. Note

is taken, then note no longer taken, then (what shall we call it)(history) the

massive chitter coming on—(singleness now truly gone)—massive and

more or less (to the human ear) the same pitch and

duration, only this time a serious

proposal, meaning to stick—formal, ruthless, kind, strange, flaring—

then suddenly crawling maggotlike around

a single hammering-sound—succession, more succession—our listening

replacing almost all the silence now, unaware of

division, past differentiation, no single

object but the hammer in the sun behind the fence,

tappings hardening and softening, and always

full hits, after which silence tumbling down as if a birdsong without

song, a mind of space making of itself a wide existence,

nothing else. Wind silks the fronds. They move

their rippling under the harshness of the festival.

Everything seems easily born. All without echo. No souvenir.

Hands everywhere full of nothing, yet very full.

Hard prize feeling hard-won out to the very edges of the visible—

full sun—(a buzz-saw now, just once, then once

again—its rise, quick fall, pushed deep into the chittering—

and then again the chittering poured into seepages and leaks),

(one gust of wind right into it),

(pushing up around the buzz and filling in

                    each emptiness).

Elsewhere things stop. Elsewhere

there is direction and things go along it and then stop.

Elsewhere motions towards good, or depth, or

elsewhere's elsewhere. Here in the hive of sun,

only the toothy present moment lives. Widening its grin.

A broom sweeps off the concrete ledge.

Two phrases spoken by the sweeper as she turns

                    her head.

Listen: between the words, the sweep,

the strands' accumulating hiss, the water dripping from the

upheld hose, low-pressure of the water's fall,

the mingling of the yellow and *the yellowest*: a power, a blind and un-

                                    important

power, but, because capable of being *all,*

still a heroic power. Even un-

vectored, even untrue.

VIA NEGATIVA

Gracious will. Gracious indistinct.

Everything depends on the point where nothing can be said.

From there we can deduce how

from now on nothing will be like.

Here lies: a border then the un-

just. Do I have, for example,

a heart? Does it only *feel* if you make "sense" of me?

Can it, for example, make me "see"?

Can it make me not see?

That we shall never know, of each other now, more.

That there is a no more. Hot and singular.

Surrounded by our first-persons: the no-more.

Before death's obligatory plurality.

But I do know you by heart.

Also know other things by heart.

Interior, spiral, damnation, your name.

What would be the opposite of "you"?

When I "think," it is near the future, just this

                     side of it.

Something I can't conceive of without saying *you*.

The desert is fueled. My desert is fueled.

Daybreak a chaos in which things first come forth

                  then mix

as in an oasis, thirsty

for distinguishment.

Then the angels who need bodies to walk in.

Then something breaking light further as in: "it came to

                     pass," or

the way my words, encountered, are canceled,

especially if true, and how they insist on encounter:

finally: in the world: "the impossible": "the little":

"in the house over there": "elsewhere than here":

what is this (erasure)(read on) is it a warning:

omit me: go back out: go back in: say:

no way to go in: go in: measure:

the little fabric vanishes, ascends, descends, vanishes,

say twenty seconds, say wall

(at the same time there is a specific temperature)

(so that eventually the light goes down all the lights go out

together)

(till the level is reached where a fall begins)(more or less

long)

SURF

All day there had been clouds and the expectation
of sun. It could "break through" anytime, they said.
It wouldn't be a large expense, they said.
And can we still use the old materials—
remembrance (bright
patch), the sound of the surf like a laden car pulling out
over gravel, so slowly, in the middle of last night,
headlights kept off, *everywhere* still expected to happen.
She felt the gloom of that architecture:
the plans of the as-yet-unbuilt,
and how sad it was, the young feeling of the middle of the
                                        night,
in it that pulling-away: as if it were really open, the elsewhere: as if
                                we could pull right into it—
the "free" the radio had called it earlier before all stations but the one
went off the air. The surf was also really there.
Behind the gravelly pulling-away into the hope of
manyness: many *kinds* [or will we all
                    be alone
together?], many *outcomes,* many luscious *vacancies*
still happily clothed in the silky "for better or
for worse." Through the windowpanes she thought she saw
things being handled by long white-gloved arms, flowers
placed strategically. The car pulls-out to "have
experiences" [the gravel's motion with like-sound of surf in it, and in it, too,
                            the actual surf
                            beyond]

until—once out the entranceway—the lights snap on and cast
apparently frantic but actually (unfortunately) random

> (except for

> forwardness)

beams through the woods.
There is, of course,
a place this will
"end up." Even the mind in the house drinking this in
knows this, how the distance can feel "crossed," yes,
how the thinking tracking it quickens,
a kind of laughter, brushing all the carefully-made plans away—
an abrupt exhalation—as if over dust.
Kind people, from time to time, at the edges of
things. Inside, a plain white wall giving one
a feeling of truth. Things waiting in mind to be placed upon it.
Like a cool drink upon it. Things laid on it in such a way
they come to be, finally, *without use.*
Soon *day* again (she thought) you can't just pick up in the middle.
She could hear the surf behind the wind-in-the-trees now that

> the car, in its secrecy,

had left [she had heard it turn,
take the two curves and, like small

> talk in

> the distance,

become distance]. Then wind, the surf, and she was sure
the car was beyond range.
It has *disappeared,* she thought, watching her lit room lay itself into

> the surrounding woods,

letting all the deviating paths and openings lead to the un-

> relenting surf

"ever receding, ever deferred" she thought, looking at the

silk-black panes.

Was she meant to see in? Was she meant to look back in at

"our"

selves (room, lamp, sea-green bedspread).

How should she spend this poverty, she thought, looking at the panes

across the room, as if they held some *truth* in the way

they faced apparently *in* (reflecting

us) while being actually a facing-*out*. They're re-

presenting each to each [she thought].

She listened over and over as if to *see* by that listening.

She tracked backwards to the last audible bit of tire on

gravel, listening for the trying-to-get-out-

unheard. It was all still there. And now, louder still, over it,

each wave of surf against which she would play the terms

"happy" "aghast" "uselessness" "perfect"

as if her mind could bend its dowsing wand

into those waves, into those waves' waves, into the foreign part of the "soul"

that was still—(there in each individual break on shore, each rise

or fall

in pitch)—

what she could call "her" soul.

Is there so much foreign matter in it? Doesn't it *belong* re-

gardless?

Blurring, yes, but alive with separateness?

To know what is coming she thought, as if to pull day-break on.

That we are moving ... She thought of the car on the highway's

dangerous and graceful resolutions—

saw its static lights and *speed* as if it were just

patience—

the escape from "here" a resolute giving-in to patience—
the patience of story—that we are moving
(looking at the mullioned squares of black for story to break
                                in them)(erasing
the room reflected there, in all its parts, again and again)
each pane placing her at a
                        slightly different angle, yes,
[somebody else's car going by terribly fast
                    down the main road]
[a conflagration of utmost nearness, appearance and
                    disappearance on either
side] the panes in sets of eight where the window still
                            holds night
[as if something out there is just waiting for you to laugh
out loud][to break][like bending to take the long expected
                        drink of water—
the long "cool" drink of water she thought because of the shiny
                        surface of the panes—
our faces as if hiding in them, in the
room in them, in the surface on the surface that must not
be looked past]. There is no plural of "change" she thought.
Or "thirst."

BY THE WAY

She slept in the wind, she was learning to sleep

                    in the wind.

This in the old city, late in the season.

For me the world is created [she would think].

Am nothing more than ashes and dust [would think].

The day encircling her sleeping seemed to even *smell* of

                            truth.

It was committed to using the past.

Thought: what am I supposed to save.

Thought: what am I supposed to remember.

Day was filled as usual with room.

In it the visible, increasingly, its devalued

                  currency.

All things seemed to be falling

under the rubric of *possessions.* All

things—as if under an invisibly descending mote-filled

mantle—trickling, full of itself—the light beams still straw-colored

holding the motes so gently as they made their way down

                          over all

things in their luscious but adamant diagonals.

This is where the painters found them, at these

steepnesses—ascent, descent—hovering,

        beautiful of

        course the

feeling—neither happy nor sad—that pleasantness the

                  soul (so

                  gradually filtered down)

throwing away the only world that would have saved them.
Is it possible [thought] to have
experience? Can I see what there is? It was

easier to

ask, for

example "to save one's self is to save what?" But she
(because of the wind perhaps)[it is this wind she thought]
began to feel there was a warning sounding—how
odd it should be so inaudible—as if a stranger from
a long time ago were appearing in a clearing—no, [thought], as

if a

clearing from long ago appeared in the stranger—in it the hissing
what-is-there [was nobody listening?][or even looking]
[and it seems unserious, truly, her throttling this
point][the stranger able to be herself—or *in*

herself]

[not as lovers though, but as a clearing that folds inside itself

body upon body that has

traversed it]

[the whole community][each self
climbing so gently over the next]—the clearing,
with its patches of dappling at the edges and long clear axial

shafts

moving all day around the center,
as a sundial would stir the day but with an element of

stubborn volition,

slant beams tracking prey at the clearing's core.
Meanwhile is one name for the clearing in-

side [at the conductive

inside of] all

[*86*]

the living—lost and unlost. *Distinction* another, as

each soul cards itself from its former and its follower.

All this time they have been waiting.

Then *thinking* (the wind that keeps the clearing open). But not

                              "thinking" as we

know it. Not to push everything back into the

                    surrounding

forest. Not to arrive at *finish* at the end.

[The end of what, she thought]

Yes there was life in the surrounding "forest."

Which filled each of the selves to their edges,

                    hazy with fullness,

restless with hard attention, fruition,

(they were, after all, always all hunting)

(the wind driving the scent sometimes this way some

                         times that)

(*outcome* the essential love of the edges, of being)—

But once the mind ended, as it were,

a wholly separate mind felt the wind of the

                    clearing.

There is no foreground in it, for instance, once this is in you, or

                         you in it—

it surrounds everything like a clear idea—

birds flying up out of its edges, dipping through it perhaps, but

                         always retreating.

Now you can enter your clearing: dazzling

imagination: eternal-looking with much thistle-down:

wild onion in the notional (hello, goodbye) stroking

                    of late light:

it grows heavy with emptiness: more wind:

you now in wind (imagine) and this wind in you.

Around you all eras have ended—progress, achievement,

opinion,

the spot where some ruler could be made to stand

exactly, signifying. Even the light-motes seem to say

[exactly]: what is an *explanation?*

People come and go in the clearing digging graves, that's

true. People are buried, slowly, systematically, in every part of it—it

takes

[and yes, at the start it *was* a flower garden]

time. But without the sense of continuity (there are

small butter-colored butterflies) without the sense of

arrangements making up a thought.

More birds fly through. Through the "she" of the

beginning

whose clearing this "you" is in. The I stands

deepening.

As a fruit ripens. For the summer of the clearing is long

once you enter the first person, bearing out-limbs, carrying

fruit.

There is no looking-back on anything.

The leaves ruffle, restless for the new.

Deeper-in yet, a worried continuing does direct

the passage of time with unnerving ease.

And yes it is important to use your mind to place the

vast analogies of cities all round this readiness.

They have to grindingly cohere

and day come round them, tightening the free.

The circulation of the versions of each instant, too (as the motes

do) strengthening

the fabric

of the surround.

All is disguised of course.

The sun on the parkbench could be a baby

girl,

the meaning in this tone of voice could be the

meant

or where a century of sleep coheres and sticks—

however momentarily. It is important.

Questions can be asked out here, in the layering

surround—

shedding the versions as a dome sheds each instant

of the given—

as if it were merely too slippery—time—and couldn't stick and so

must pass . . .

The dome of the city: how it seems to rise up out of nothingness

with dawn, and rise into perennial noon, and rise

just this

much further at

the sudden end of noon—an upper story—pulled up by

ropes of

human glance—and shedding, continuously shedding

day. Something grows over it.

Something displaced by its [imagined] rising-up. Something

something fills-in

in the wake of that dis-

placement, yes. Jays overheard now quarrelling, then dropping—

three—

into my shadow, now. Me watching how it's chained to me

as they

hop back and forth, clearing my darkening as if to step

free of a

thought. Hard thought. Free, and then re-

entering. Until the clearing (as if overheard in

                        the next room)

(in the voices of others that change

without explanation) rises

again, inside, so near, in the mind, neither in foreground nor in back,

light flowing suddenly more freely there where the edges

                        are, and the clearing

                        itself

is entered—look: there is no one way to go—

light floods a bit, one feels a center, all directions shine from it,

[is a center sought?] I mean, because I'm one of the

few, you know, right here for you,

going on like this, in America,

where the dream is of course gone because it has

too much power, one of the few,

hiding from disbelief,

and it's not a dark place, you know, though so inward,

and it takes up all the room.

V

THE TAKEN-DOWN GOD

(Easter Saturday, Chapel of Maria-Santa)

You are not supposed to write in the presence so I can't really do
this task [*for us*] in there [feel fear when I feel for my pen][in pocket][have
come outside, sit on the steps, people watching me as they
go in][remember]: in there: children who can't see told to kiss a
wooden hand: me watching them feel for it: elongated 18th-century fingers like
washboarded ocean-floor: tide-action grooved-in: mile after mile of the fingers
of the hand of the god, a puppet, larger than life, highly muscled, loose
at the joints, who has been made here [now] to lie down, in our
midst [now], small velvet bed [grave], knee-high to us,
naked, still, of wood, pain [in the face], crown that doesn't come off, thorns
steel, white-gauze wedding veil over the length of him, through which
the small coughs of the weeping seem not
to cross, mosquito netting really—they have made him the bride of
our dirt-waiting, dirt-watching—no—they have whitened the ardent darkening
of his [from which blood trickles] chest, the veil made to seem a great load: our gaze
caught up on it: trawled up in that netting: trawled from the famished
wedding-sea. Oh swim. What are you carrying. You must
jettison it now.

*

Look up, the cross is empty. There are holes on the wall in the
sky where he was, where he will go tomorrow. Usually the children who are
brought will cry. Nervously one puts the money in the little box.
The canopy over him is held by pulleys [gold]. The tassels are made
                                        tremulous by

entrances and exits through the half-open door. And by the coughs or
shushed-up laughs, here and there, of lifted kids. When the bells begin
you can taste the metal on the evening air. It is the only thing
that seems to cross the netting. Iron. Iron as in: women, eyes red, holding
all children still. Look: one runs loose and is not caught in time. The veil is
clenched and ripples where he, in falling, grabs-on, falls, then is picked up
in time, the boy-god's body tilting to one side, thighs wavering, trunk slow, as if
                                        now drifting, now
sinking—how deep the water of the watching is—net sliding off—he seems to
                                        free himself—then all
is rectified.

                                    *

"They gasp." "But one child laughs out loud." "The now." Why are these words
                                        an insult to
the god? Especially if written down. Why this notation on this page a
rip? Presence. Forgive me [I have taken this pad indoors][am sitting in
a tiny pew] I mean to be among the women who surround the god and weep.
They bend and kiss the feet. More coughs. Yes, the speaking subject in
                            me wants
to rip the veil. Thought "if I bring my pen to bear inside something
will rip." But what? We write. We would like to live somewhere. We wish to
                                        take down
what will continue in all events to rise. We wish to not be erased from the
picture. We wish to picture the erasure. The human earth and its appearance.
The human and its disappearance. What do you think I've been about all this
                                        long time,
half-crazed, pen-in-hand, looking up, looking back down, taking it down,
taking it *all* down. Look it is a burning really. See, the smoke

rises from the altar. And, too, there is the rising that attaches itself to a [veiled] thing:
what seems to rise off all sides of the lain-down, hand-made [god]. We

*

would like to say there is *somewhere* from which we are taken to which

we will be

taken. Ruin, in here, grows sweet. The sweetness seems to rise to cover
everything. I have written in this manner, rapidly, scratching, hearing them hear
this constant incompletion as it tries to *be* (softly as possible) over this page.
Look, they look at me. Some from praying look. The upglance cast
gets into this sentence. Also I hear the chickadees. Also some doves outside.
I exaggerate them. Birdcall against stone wall: etruscan: roman: romanesque:
gothic: birds blistering, up in the archways, finding purchase,
carrying back and forth the bits of twig and something white. From here I'd say
it is a piece of veil—but it was plastic from a shopping bag. We
would like someplace to "live." This appears to you as a photo? This appears to you
as a voice? Bodiless or headless? The shadow of which part of the whole?
Human? The illustration of? A metaphysical impossibility—I can hardly conceive of
you, out there, as I squint you in. Voice and address and attention and in-
attention. Sparkling, in here, the light cracks-down against the walls from
the single, high-up-above-the-altar, window. Like chips of rock, this light

thrown against walls

according to the laws of the broken and the unbroken and
the breaking.

*

The parentlight above this town: curious: one thing: no idea: what virtue
attends it? We value style. No, we are the keepers of a flame called

[95]

style. I'm holding it in my right hand. Look—it has such fluency.
The other sounds in here are: currency folded and slid into the little 18th
century box: the cane on the floor clicking in, then later out: the heels of
shoes on stone where the prayer stands in place for a long time: the muttering
where words are cast out into the empty air of the enclosed place:
the whispering which is a different kind of prayer: the sniffling:
birdcries which the open door lets in: the kissing: how the veil
slips and slides over the unmoving beauties of the dead wood boy:
the curious hum of trapped-in light: also more birdcalls: also the call of one
outside trying to find someone: also the second, louder call, trying to catch that one
in time: a name: the (high-pitched) call: unreached, then

                                       reached, a
human attention: and beyond that: the hurrying: the creatures that keep
out of sight: fields, hedgerows, trees: all laying-low their nets of sound
to catch the absence. It

                       *

is caught. Yes—possession—but of another kind. I promise you. My pen is
a bypath. It has come in from outside. It is colossal, the tiny sound it makes
as I insist in here. How quilled these explanations of absence are as they
group round. Are these sentences full? Are they fresh, as the April air outside
is fresh [near dusk][swallows now beginning to feed]. Thinking appears as
words. "Gli Stati Uniti rifiutano gli accordi di Kyoto—addio
al mondo" [this serves as that which dates the *here*]. Weren't we here? Wasn't I
in here? And you here too? We have "written"—can't you feel it
in your hands [this pen for instance, this scratchy weightlessness] or in your
eyes [the incense filling up this church] or mind ["at the summit of the tiny
hilltop town"]—haven't our eyes the empty cross before them now: here:

*

in this [real time] between us [if you will do the work]: a wall, frescoed,

with fading gold and lesser-yellow trim (pastoral imagery made into

pattern in the trim). And at the center of the emptiness (vertical)(rectangular)

this absence: blue (all over)(no horizon), a brownish empty cross, frescoed wall itself

cut-into in

hundreds of spots, some gouges deep, as if white birds are flying through—swoops,

dips—

long scratches where the arms are taken down and put back up each year—also two

soldiers, weight to one hip: a stance: their looking up at

him [not there]: each leaning on a lance: also two holes

at the far edges of the horizontal plank, large screwjoints where he gets

braced-back, one near the bottom of the vertical, black in those holes where

shadows

pool. There: a picture: the ruin of the mind: did you not *make* it?: because you

can, you

really can: you only have to want to: now

*

a voice will say "Father"—but, no: there is nothing: the

voice will say father meaning by that nothing: now

these words will say "you"—but, no: there is nothing: these

words will say you meaning by that dear nothing: now

this pen will say raise up the man, pull back

the veil, slide it off to the side, meaning by that dear nothing, now

this voice which is called "I" will say to you: now:
now: [can you do *that?*]: now: [do you feel it][there in

your face, in your palms]: *now*: [doesn't it still you][put
birdchatter in][put dusk-wind in olive groves "below"]: now:

we are done we are alone we are a dialect but it can still be
spoken: there is a literal edge: now: there are

facts, too, yes: now: where were we: sliding the veil aside which is
easy, it pulls off with one sweep, it surrenders the body: now

the surround is you: the moment: the [birdcries in it] next
moment and the next: yet now: always still the now: always

still: the body: lift it back up (it will take two of you)
(it is about eight feet): this thought in you: this pen I scour

this church clean with, me on the rickety straw-plaited seat: this
like a full moon preparing to come up in you: all the

tides [raise the globe an instant: the oceans: the *one end* and the *other* of them:
the *center* of: the *bottom* of]: you the litigant

now in this high court: you being asked to argue the case: you: you: now:
strange and low the sensation in you as you lift the slippery wooden

creature

back onto its place, being handed the screwdriver, turning it slowly with your
right hand, left hand holding the center piece (the chest) flat up

against the wall: endless erasure: long calm: long dangerous what-ifs:

and the path: promising both angles: always both: *the* both [*up*

and *down*]

though only *out* once you go out this door.

HIGH TIDE

She held a sign that said Emergency [nothing else].
Handwritten in pencil on the corrugated strip of boxtop.
Everywhere someone's dreams are realized.
Everywhere memory slicks its pebble back and forth at the bottom of
                                                its riverbed,
like happiness drifting over what *exists*,
always "close" to its mark—always almost just-within
                        the charmed circle of yes of
what happened—yes.
Over and over the same one spot, drifting near target, recreating the
                                        target,
what was it we were talking about, the circle, the circle of our
                                lost
x, forgetting and remembering in the same instant. I came ever closer. I
                                        began. I
wrote my name firmly. Extruded meaning—unmistakable
thing.

*

Where was I? It was winter. There where it rolls forward then
stops. The god or gods were not overt. The day [their
habitation] veiled. [Gods disappear at night][One of the
mysteries]. She: a woman of sixty: long gray and
matted hair, many grays, also some blue in it: no light received or
                                fed back by

her skin: and talking all day to the forever-descending in-

visible,

in the dome of listening, in hearing, in the invincible

ministering: talking as if tasting of something on air [frost,

host] and always rocking slightly back and forth—until one is finally

alongside her—

walking by—rags upon rags wrapping her—the whole city's buzzing

code [the one that takes "forever" to transmit] around her,

her rolling and tossing her head, the steam from her lips

lifting blue off her tongue [you can see tongue][sometimes even

back of throat] and growing more silent as I

approach: two women: one holding one word [all caps] up [torn gloves, wool layers

frazzling][moving her eyes as I move away]: then street: then

abstraction of her: then her back there laughing once out loud,

me tossing a quick glance up at the sky, me crossing

the street. I feel scribbled-in. Something inattentive has barely

written me in.

*

Every day I walk by. She is a door with her inscription, I

go by. I look in as if I have nothing to fear, I

walk by. I cross her gaze. We lock in thought, of that I am

sure. Her face cants a bit to peer at me. There is

no identifiable cause and no identifiable

effect. There is no flexibility between hearts. There might be

between minds, I'm not sure. None in the linked-up

gaze. Much in the remembering [gaze on my back

laid hard at first then weakening as I go somewhere I

am due]. All this is in this sentence. Also in
the fractures where periods are placed. You the listener are or are not
expendable, I don't know, I'm not sure. A couple of
days "go by." It seems this could take forever. It seems this
should take Forever into its garb, deep into its folds, and wrap and
wrap it, holding us firm. Firm enough to make
fear not so hurried, there at our faces, there at
our backs.... So I come close to her.
It takes form and time. Who would have expected it
would end this way. The journey out.

*

Once after high-tide along south beach I found a beachlong
                                        scripting
of debris: seaweeds of various thicknesses and drynesses, all
intertwined, some wrappers, shiny, bleached—
strips of mylar, flimsier [translucent] plastic blues—yarn, twine—spines of
                                        strange bits of
fish, and carapaces—parts of birds or were they shells—
actual glass and fishing lures that looked like glass—
all grained-up in the sand and clay that
swirled-up round in ground-winds—nothing extruding—
all woven tight and rolled and braided-up: that's
what I saw hang every morning round her head, but long,
and not just gray but taupes and browns—sometimes some shells,
and always strands that looked like wool. Nearby
her rolled-up sleeping bag and other bags. A liquid thing,
her *here*. Yet also thick. If I get very close,
I feel a wish between us like
a silver thing. Sadness, yes, in our

one gaze [at certain points as you

approach it becomes one][the ends of each long

separation

knit][right there] also the scent of blue [oncoming snow] also

hard snow

already on the ground, also

wonderment also bafflement also still air.

*

Late November, five a.m., walking back from the emergency

room, prescription in hand, ice on the empty trees, I see her

sleeping there, her long thick grouped-up hair over the brick

sidewalk,

the top fold of the sleeping bag flapped back

by strong ground-gusts. Her cheek, exposed,

looks too much more than cold.

I cross the street. Bending, gently as I can, to fold

the blue flap back over the freezing face, wind rattling wildly in my

paper sack, my face blown flat with cold—ache

even in the fingers, even in the eyes—accidentally

I graze her cheek. So far does the mind go, I fill

with the sensation of having

goodness—actual goodness?—fill with my

thinking it good

out to the very edges of my hand—touching her cheek—feel love?: it's not

a cheek, it's paste—or gum and some admixture—

pull the hair back and it's not hair, it's wool and phloxed-up

random yarns, old woolen caps stuffed in a stocking

face, with gum laid on—or is it latex paint—onto

the cheek, making a chin: it is a puppet: it is a place

holding a place: it is an eclipse of: of holding
on: of *on*: or *in*: or what a *here* can be
                if what one is

is finally reduced to *here*: it is *not* "now": that's what's

been taken elsewhere now: strange splitting of this
atom: her in my mind as it bends down to

feel along: a seam in mesh near where the ear
would be: but running down the front, no mouth, no

hole—I seek a rip—a mark, a stitching-in—if only for the trickery—

moving back up it's only crusted lacquer tells me
it is eyes—I feel with fingertip and it flakes off, what must be

pupil painted on: must find the words: no:
must find what sparkles here, what virtue is existing

only here: my self: her self: this holding-of-place: this strict
                              eight feet of
sidewalk in America: America: you witch: dreaming always of here from an

elsewhere, from a nowhere: I'm looking through a wind that's like a wall for
a proper name: for identification: representation:

divine emptiness: it's been 21 minutes:
crashing, the wave deposits its gift: difference: indifference:

and the long sepulcher: identity: open: *meanwhile* in the arms of
elsewhere: someone has pushed the rock aside: I see

the loan: I see its terms (maybe): I see the payable and
the unpayable: the open-ended credit: created: equal: look.

RELAY STATION

There is [in truth] a highest tide each year—
yes—there are many things—words that come *and* go—

things that are *kept*—[these all high tides]—or where there is
                                                    [as if]
a partly open door [of sorts] through which some of
                                    the residue of

origin can, broken off from source, ride, just a little higher, deeper,
                                                    deeper-in,
in-through. In truth, there is, in grammar,

something where one is truly *one*—link by link,
crystalline—

into which [through which] the voice can empty and refract
what has been seen, or thought, or thought to have been seen,

or to have been. Sometimes one's hopes are "realized."
Sometimes, just before the highest tide's one, single, highest wave
                                                    retreats,

a thing and its description *can* be one: can be *the time it takes to say the
thing*. The thing. Laid right down there in "the word," down, as a weight in
                                                    its weight,
down—[lord as if garnished with laurel]—[more on that later but
                                    for now

this]—until here it is: the cargo: [arrival][stressful][yes][as any singleness is][a
                                                    star][a

bird][a caught thing in a web just now ceasing to stir]—laid
down as the abstract-sense is laid onto the thing—[not as these actual bees

covering this hill, but as the *hum*][an ache over the thing][the rising and
                                        slightly enlarging
                                        change of its
nature][formal][it was going to take

forever][words the first act][such a liquid thing the first act]["the point"]

[the correctness of it]—then *eternity!* How one expected, rising and
                                        lowering with
these tides, for it to keep making its cameo appearance: what one saw from

the suddenly uplifted rise of a wavetop, for instance: quick: through: not like
a dream no: not even fever no: even from here knowing it to be painstaking: e-
                                        laborated:

directing everything forward onto shoreline, expectant, never anything but
                                        expectant,
pushed forever from behind.

NOTES

PRAYER ("minnows") was written as a turn-of-the-millennium poem for the *New York Times* Op-Ed page, and was originally dated 12.31.00

EVOLUTION ("How old are you?"): some of the questions were provided by the questionnaire the *New York Times* used in conducting the poll the results of which were given me as an "assignment" for this poem. An additional fact, which reached me while I was writing this poem, struck me: during the 1850s, while Darwin was concluding *On the Origin of Species*, the rate of extinction [for species] is believed to have been one every five years. Today, the rate of extinction is estimated at one every nine minutes. Throughout the writing of this book, I was haunted by the sensation of that nine-minute span—which might amount to the time it takes to read any poem here before you. My sense of that time frame [and its inevitable increase, even as we "speak"] inhabits, as well as structures, the book. It is written up against the sensation of what is now called "ecocide." I was also influenced by, among other texts, the "World Scientists' Warning to Humanity," sponsored by the Union of Concerned Scientists (1993).

PRAYER ("From Behind Trees"): the last line is loosely based on a line of Zbigniew Herbert's in his prose-poem "Cernunnos" (from *Elegy for the Departure*). I take my poem to be in conversation with such notion of the gods—and of how history transforms them—as is put forth in Herbert's poem. In attempting to enact a realistic description of metamorphoses, "Prayer" wonders, among other things, what the "suitable" distance between subject and object, gods and humans, humans and nature, might indeed be.

ESTUARY: some parenthetical fragments of facts are taken from *The Year 1000: What Life Was Like at the Time of the First Millennium* by Robert Lacey (Danny Danziger, 1999).

KYOTO owes a debt to Gary Snyder in its second and third line, and is dedicated to him.

SOLITUDE: some language—especially individual terms—is taken from Darwin, using the Norton Critical Edition, selected and edited by Philip Appleman, as well as from Merleau Ponty's *The Visible and the Invisible* (Alphonso Lingis, translator, North-western University Press, 1968).

THE TAKEN-DOWN GOD: the tiny church in Umbria, Italy, where this takes place is not given its actual name in the subtitle. The phrase in the sixth section, taken from an Italian newspaper headline, translates as "The United States refuses the Kyoto Accords—farewell to the world."

ABOUT THE AUTHOR

Jorie Graham is author of eight collections of poetry, including *The Dream of the Unified Field: Selected Poems 1974–1994,* which won the Pulitzer Prize. She lives in Cambridge, Massachusetts, and teaches at Harvard University.